THE DARK SIDE OF SILENCE

ORLA KELLY PUBLISHING

Raymond Poole

Dedication

This Is The Face Of War

This is the face of war
This is the face of despair
This is the face of hopelessness
This is the face of abandonment
This is the face of life
This is the face of death
This is the face of the past
This is the face of the present
This is the face of the future
This is the face of loss
This is the face of our shame

This book is dedicated to all those children across the globe who struggle on a daily basis for food, shelter, comfort, and recognition of their existence. During a time of global pandemic, while First World countries rush to vaccinate their citizens, it is important to realise that none of us are safe until we are all safe. All of the author's profits raised from the sales of this book will be donated to UNICEF Ireland to help support those children whose lives are as important as those of our children and grandchildren.

Contents

THE DARK SIDE OF

SILENCE

Raymond Poole

Preface

This book of poetry traverses a number of years and emotions covering such topics as love, loss, grief, and birth. This collection of poems are my unborn children, my orphan thoughts who now seek refuge in your hearts.

The darkness of my soul stains these brightly lit pages in the hope you may provide comfort to them. Poetry to me is the embryotic meanderings of our inner thoughts that otherwise may never see the light. They are the lost files from our lives, they are the self-opinionated conversations that otherwise fall silent under the darkness of sleepless nights. Where your inner thoughts come out to play and you find comfort in the anonymity of the night.

The elitist poets of centuries past may have frowned their furrowed intellectual brows in dismay at the lack of structure, rhyme and the total disregard for classical style or format to these poems. However, they are written by a dyslexic autistic author who makes no apologies how they are formed, rather he sees it as a celebration of his uniqueness.

Leonard Cohen once described it perfectly in an interview. He stated that no one has the right to call themselves a poet – that is for others to decide. Upon reflection, he described himself as a fraudulent poet. In many ways that is how I too would describe myself, therefore please accept this book of poetry from a fraudulent poet. I hope you will find some that cause a momentary pause of inner reflection and even perhaps self-awareness.

Foreword by Gareth O'Callaghan

William Wordsworth once said, 'Fill your paper with the breathings of your heart.' Within the pages of this book, you will find a big caring heart that beats like a shaman's drum within the words of its poetry: with love, and joy; but equally with a sense of anger, and isolation, and a sadness that too many people believe that suffering and poverty are tragedies that happen to other people somewhere else in the world, and there is nothing we can do to alleviate their plight; and yet these lovingly-crafted poems carry a bright torch that insists we must never give up on hope, because hope is the seat of the soul.

When Raymond asked me if I would write the Foreword to this deeply moving collection of his poems, I felt both honoured and slightly nervous, because poetry is so personal; it nourishes a place deep inside us, in a way that we are reminded of when we might unexpectedly hear an old poem that brings alive happy childhood memories, or a brand new poem that over time creates a different and welcomed perspective on one of life's curveballs that has been making us feel lost and anxious.

I often wonder if this special place is what I find when I focus on the silence between my heartbeats, or in the calmness of the night air that finds me, when sleep is like one of those phone numbers that leaves me on hold for what seems like forever, or in the peacefulness of an empty church that you find off the beaten track on an afternoon, and as you sit there you watch beams of warm sunlight refract as they pass through the stained-glass images. These special places provide the seeds of poetry. Poetry exists within a divine dimension: a place we enter like no other in the hope that we might make more sense of our confusing existence.

Most of us will have a brush with an illness of some form during our lifetimes here. Some of the illnesses will eventually pass, just like a long fortnight of low cloud, and rain that feels as though it will never end, and a melancholy that tears away at the ego we spend the good times hiding behind. Other illnesses will topple our finest efforts to move beyond them. They arrive unannounced, their demands are so great and so unstoppable, all that is left in their wake is devastation and grief.

Such is life, which is why I try to live every day as if it is my last, while I also try to live as though I will survive forever. One thing is for certain – when illness comes knocking, that is when your life takes on a whole new terrifying meaning. Terrifying because of the notion that blindsides you on a dark night that the days are now numbered.

The Dark Side Of Silence is a reminder of how vulnerable each of us is; but it is also a lesson about beauty and inner growth, and how they exist within that vulnerability, once we welcome it as a core part of what we are, and then immerse ourselves in it in the hope of finding out who we truly be. If we run away from our vulnerability, then we are running away from life. We cannot be truly alive unless we are truly vulnerable at the same time. Nor can we be truly alive if we lose the connection to the child each one of us once was, and, in so many ways, will always be. That child has made each of us who we are today.

One of the many poems I love in this collection is 'New Year's Eve of Life'. It is raw and visceral in its images, and in questions we ask ourselves at some point of the journey. I found it difficult to catch my breath as I read it. Each question demands an honest answer – the same level of honesty we expect from our children: "Is one life of greater or lesser importance than another?" It does not make for gentle reading, nor should it, because our vacuous society needs a wake-up call. "This life, this world, this hypocrisy we perform, we care for others only if they care for us." This is a poem that I hope some day to see on the State exams, because we need to acknowledge that the lives of others matter; and then there is that killer line that makes so many look the other way so fast, they could get whiplashed: "Refugees are not welcomed as we forget our history." When we lose sight of others who need our support, we also lose sight of ourselves. Resentment destroys our ability to love.

Too many of us live our short lives vicariously, listening to other people's opinions in order to form our own opinions. We do not want to be perceived as being different, as the ones standing out from the crowd. We hate drawing attention to ourselves. If Covid has taught us anything, it is this: there is only one certainty in this life, and that is there are no certainties.

None of us lives alone on an island; yet so many people today build their homes to resemble an inaccessible island, surrounding them with high, fortified and fenced walls, locking out the world, preferring to talk to 'the outsiders' by way of a speaker attached to the tall electric iron gates. This is self-imposed isolation that tries to keep vulnerability at a safe distance. They are not locking out strangers, they are trying to lock out vulnerability. But when illness, or poverty in its many camouflaged guises comes calling, no amount of security or self-imposed solitude will protect them.

Raymond Poole is not afraid to speak about how he feels, and about how he deals with a life that has left some very challenging hurdles on his doorstep; but it is his fearless vulnerability in the face of these life-threatening challenges that have made him someone unique, someone who I try never to miss an opportunity to listen to, because he always makes me feel better and stronger in those moments when the pain of illness makes no sense, and the familiar voices of people who you thought would be there for you have made excuses not to be.

All of life is laid bare on the pages of this stunning collection of personal givens, and painful echoes, and reminders that we will never fully figure out this life we have been given the chance to be a short part of. Of course, we can learn. That is an unspoken part of the reason why we are here; namely to learn about who we truly are. Most of us fail to see the point in that until something goes horribly wrong.

We are only visitors passing through. We can never permanently lay claim to anything in our lifetimes, other than the love we have shown to others, and the lasting impressions we have made on their lives. And finally on that note, another favourite poem is 'The Garden Bench', which reminds me each time I go back to it, "Your presence in this life is not measured by what you do, but rather the enormity of the void you leave behind."

Take this beautiful collection of poems to heart; spend even ten minutes each day allowing the words to transport you to places where your kindness and empathy will be welcomed with open arms, and in turn given back to you a hundredfold.

Gareth O'Callaghan,

July 2021

WAXING CRESCENT

The Dark Side Of Silence

What is light without darkness?
Is it not simply an unwanted constant?
No sunset nor sunrise simply light
An aperture of blindness
Darkness becomes light's resting ground
A period of recuperation

For in darkness we find our new dawn
A new day born with hope
As Hope only sits at the table of Despair
But to be saved, first we must fall
Spiralling out of control to the marshlands
Where our feet are weighed down by our insignificance

Sorrows salted tears are always the sweetest
Lost abandoned love circumventing ecstasy
The kiss on the lips of desire
Passion skipping heartbeats
Only to vaporise in a momentary lapse
As the faceless faces turn back to snare

3

In the darkness we patiently wait
The dark side of silence enters
Where fears playout their turmoil
And hope springs forth
The darkness now succumbs to the light
Bowing as it departs in acknowledgement
To their coexistence and interdependency

Seahorses

Frantically fumbling in the darkness on the open sea
Searching for the safety of my mother's embrace
She's nowhere to be found in the bleakness of the night
Clambering to catch my breath as the water engulfs my lungs
The salt of my tears meld with the salt of the sea
I hear the wave's crash around me as I slowly sink down
Spiralling into the abyss of my murky grave
Once again I am surrounded by water as I was at birth
And like at birth no one on the outside can hear my cries
I am carried upon the mane of the seahorses
Discarded at the ebb of the beach like a washed up piece of garbage
We came in search of sanctuary, freedom and compassion
There were no doors open to us, no helping hands outstretched
Now my family and I are silent, we burden you no more
We seek no refuge, no safe harbour
You need not divert your glances from the view of my still body
Our burdensome presence is no longer your concern
Like you I too will sleep soundly tonight
However, I shall never awaken to see the break of dawn
My image is now a scar upon your caring society
And as that scar heals, my life's worth is erased
Our names once written into the sands of time
Disappear as the tide once again goes out
We were parted at sea only to be reunited within the refuge of death
The white seahorses vanquished on the sea of life
Society's balance restored whilst you kneel before your God

5

As your faith guides you, justifying your existence and extinguishing ours
Seahorses drowned upon the parting sea as no passage to safety existed

This poem is dedicated to the memory of Aylan Kurdi, may he and his family rest in peace.

What If...

What if I screamed my silent cries aloud, would you think me mad?
What if I gave up, would you think me sad?
What if I didn't exist, would you miss me?
What if I asked for a hug, would you think me needy?
What if I was just me, would you still love me?
What if I never spoke of my fears, would you think me brave?
What if I said how I truly feel, would you listen?
What if I asked for forgiveness, would you forgive me?
What if, it had all never happened?

A Father's Unspoken Love

The thick black rimmed glasses
Providing that Michael Caine persona
For the man who rarely uttered the words, "I love you"
Mum would explain
How you found them difficult to say
Then later in life those barriers rose
When despair crossed my door
You found the courage to utter them
I reached out with my aching heart
Grappling for strength within your eyes
"You know I love you dad" I whimpered
"I do," then that never ending momentary pause
Before confirmation of your love
"I love you too"
Simple small words with magnitude of meaning
Acknowledgement of reciprocal feelings
His generation was that of stunted emotions
Wrapped within a barbed wire of self-isolation
Seeking a reprieve from emotional constipation
Only to arrive in the autumn of life
Their love never doubted but rarely uttered
Their life's lesson became our tutor
Now as the ticking of the clock
Reverberates throughout the hollow room
The scent of your aftershave lingers in the air
The echo chambers within my head
Fading with the passing of time
I listen intently to capture those words
"I love you"

Goodnight My Father

The deafening sound of silence
The awkwardness of death
He hovers across the sterile floor
Seeking his repayment
Patiently waiting for his moment of retribution
Eighty five years he's bided his time
Frequently knocking to no avail
Tonight he crawls silently into your room
Like the early morning fog
Forming a white veil upon your bed
No footsteps heard, no sound made
Harvesting the breath of your life
As your body lays still
Ever watching, never menacing
I hold your hand, he lightens your grip
Grasping tighter, I selfishly linger momentarily
The son becomes the parent
The parent the child
Sleep well my father, you fought hard
She has waited patiently for you
Separated in life, now you will be reunited in death
It's time to go, no regrets, no anger
You loved and were loved
Goodnight my father

Life's Gateway

There stands a crooked gate with life's soil trodden pathway leading
through it
The morning dew barely vaporised by the rising sun
As it lingers seductively above inviting you to enter
The air is filled with the anticipation of memories yet to be born
It is the gate of our future, the pathway of opportunities
Expeditions of life yet to be explored
As we enter we leave behind our life of old
Shedding mistakes, regrets, heartaches and misgivings
But we carry forth those cherished memories we hold dear
We are filled with anticipation of new beginnings
Friendships, encounters, experiences yet to be lived
It is the dawn of a new birth as we leave behind the summer of our
youth
Autumn is here, the myriad of golden leaves hang tentatively on the
tree of life
The warmth of your breath lingers in the air as you whisper your love
for me
Hands entwined we walk side by side through the gate never to be
parted
Till winter comes knocking we shall comfort one another and stay off
the frost of time
As we pause momentarily to look back we move forward full of
vigour for life yet to be lived

New Year's Eve Of Life

I am not old but yet my body is slowing me down
Momentarily passing glances in the mirror show someone else
The person I knew myself to be is passed
My eyes deceive me as they look out from this vessel
The voices in my head sound familiarly youthful
I once shone brightly now I glisten
Like an ember from the fire of life
I shot forth shining intensely
Only to burn out and disappear into the darkness of death
My skin no longer fits me like a tight glove
Rather the tightness and elasticity has faded
Now my skin lies loosely upon the frame of my aching bones
As I sailed the waves on the sea of life
I find myself cast overboard being dragged to the depths of
mediocrity
Shackled by the insignificance of my futile existence
Drowning in my self-pity I see the reflection of what could have been
The life that should have but for the distraction of self-indulgence
As I pass I no longer hear my name mentioned
Time will erase my futile existence from this life
Memories left behind will fade upon the passing of one generation
I lived for what, to do what, for whom
Am I truly alive or simply passing time to serve my Master, death?
Who am I to question the meaning of life?
Is there a meaning to life?
Is one life of greater or lesser importance than another's?
Is intelligence truly defined by academic ability?

Is empathy not more important than scholarly musings?
Has our surroundings and experiences defined what we've become
Where is the child within that was carefree?
The child that skipped as they walked
The child who was hungry for knowledge
The child who cried openly
The child who laughed loudly
The child who gave love unconditionally
Am I already dead if that child has left me?
Is my body simply an empty vessel of its former self?
Am I consuming time awaiting my final breath?
But yet I am not dead, I know not whether I am old
I know not the hour nor day of my demise
How then do I know if I am old?
What is old, an age, a concept, a state?
This life, this world, this hypocrisy we perform
We care for others only if they care for us
We rape the planet of its offerings to satisfy our self-indulgence
We kill one another in the name of different Gods but yet they are
one
We see wealth as monetary gain rather than the ability to care for
others
Homelessness is the status quo as politicians play with our lives
Refugees are not welcomed as we forget our history
Children die to provide us with our trinkets
The blind eye is everywhere as ignorance is our defence
My life will be short lived compared to the trees

But yet I feel I have lived long but to what avail
If I do not improve the life of others what difference is it how long
I've lived?
Now as my life passes momentarily before me I see no value in its
existence
Is it too late to change, do I want to change, why should I change
This life nay this existence is dragging me down
I'm consumed by the breadth of ignorance within and without
Does death have to mean my non-existence?
Rather I kill off that indulgent self and reborn myself from its embers
Like the Phoenix rises from the dirt to bring meaning back into life
Let me die this evening on the New Year's Eve of Life
Tomorrow I will emerge a better person
Death will be my saving grace as without it I cannot be reborn
I welcome you to my bed tonight to release the shackles
No longer will I drown in my own self indulgence
No longer will I exist for the mere sake of existence
Tomorrow will bring a new dawn to my life
One more chance to relieve my inner turmoil
One more chance to not fail my ideology
One more chance to breathe freely
Will you take this journey with me?
Or shall we die clutched in one another's arms
Sharing the breath of one another
Watching our eyes slowly fade
Feeling the grasp upon our bodies slip away
Till death do us part
Till the morning then
Till our hearts beat as one
Slowly, slowly, till stillness submits

FIRST QUARTER

The Virgin Poet

Revolution of words and expressionism
Rhythmic rhymes lay in the gutter
Sonnets squirm at the disbandment of structure
Naked words traverse the sheets
Catholic priests avert their eyes to the intercourse of transient verse
Whilst gender recognition is distorted in favour of "they"
Ejaculation of unbridled thought spurts forward
As orgasmic fever straddles the Virgin poet
Premature thoughts burst to life
Exploding a pandemic of unrestricted recourse
Words collide and verses form as neurodiversity is celebrated
The virgin poet is no longer

An Atheist Prayer

In moments of despair when loved ones suffer
What I'd give to forego my atheism
In favour of saying a prayer

But my childhood God does not exist
He was an imposed belief
My unborn atheism vilified

Replaced by a figment of imagination
A belief in the unbelievable
From a time when society
Was governed through fear

They vanquished false Gods in his favour
No longer did one adorn icons
Rather they genuflect to an image

Sin was the control of the masses
False witness punishable by death
The unmarried mother gave birth
To the son of their God

In order that all unmarried mothers
Would now give birth to original sin
Punishable by rejection of society
Their children bastardised in his name

The fisherman of men
Banished women to the lower classes
Their bodies vilified as temptresses
Little children were to suffer
As they knelt before his servants
Their innocent bodies violated

Where is their saving God now?
Turning the blind eye
No prayers for their innocent souls

The language of irreverence
Rants of hypnotic hypocrisy
Rather I keep thoughts of well-being

In my mind for my ailing friends
Than recite a rhyme to a false God
My atheist prayer of thoughts

I Never Knew I Could Say No…

Innocence raped, trust mutilated, emotional blackmail
I was but seven summers through my childhood when he came
overshadowing my innocence
The pureness of the white collar was drowned by the blackness of his
robe
Only to be equalled by the darkness of his soul

Trust was engrained through society's blindness of his stature
He stood for purity, holiness and self-sacrifice
No one told me that I was to be the sacrificial lamb
His hands soft from the lack of hard labour, crawled across my pure
innocent body

His years were three decades or more; respect your elders I heard
My body shivered, trembled at his touch, my innocence stolen
I could not run, paralysis from misaligned respect, nowhere to seek
refuge
My tears invisible to the world, my cries drowned in self-inflicted guilt

Oh please make it stop, but alas my prayer to his God would go unheard
'It will be our little secret', he whispered into my ear through his
tobacco stenched breath
I cried myself asleep not knowing why but sensing it was wrong,
I never knew I could say no…

Damaged Goods

Born to a loving family with all the imperfections that exist in a
family unit
The runt of the litter, the child who could not wait to be born
Too gentle for a boy they said, too pretty to be heterosexual
Whispers in the corridors, nudges and sly glances

Damaged goods, soiled through years of physical, mental and sexual
abuse
At the hands of the glistening white collars, societies guardians
against Satan
Struggled, stumbled, crawled his way through puberty
Mummy's boy they jeered with the spiteful venom in their tone

Slow, lazy, mentally challenged were the tag lines in school reports
Destined to roam aimlessly through life
He'll never find purpose in life, they scorned at him

Rise above she whispered, you are my gift to the universe
They know not what I do, you are my light shine bright
As out of darkness comes light

Are You There Mummy?

Sweets discarded, toys abandoned, tears cascading down my face.
It hurts so bad, make the pain go away, where are you mummy?
Safety, warmth, pain dissipates, all is good, wrapped in the comfort of your arms.

Failed exams, fearfulness, pariah of educational acceptance, tears are within.
I am sinking in the quicksand of my own inadequacies, anxiety of uncertainty, are you there mum? Hopelessness dissipates; all is good as your words of belief dispel my insecurities

Abandoned in love, paralysis of emotion ensues.
Bleakness descends suppressing the light of hope, are you there mother?
Cup of tea, favourite dinner, home baked apple pie; a mother's love is never conditional.

What to do, parenthood is overwhelming, futility at my inability to cope.
Failure has once again come knocking on the door of hope, are you there grandma?
Understanding, compassion, silence but reassurance in your ever presence of constant stability.

The youthfulness of your heart has cheated the harsh years of your journey upon your face.
I touch your cheek, we smile, no words, none needed, I hold you in my arms.
You look into my face like only a mother can, as I look back in your eyes I ask myself, are you in there mummy?

I Am...

I am strong but yet so fragile
I am brave but yet so scared
I am alive but yet void of feeling
I am surrounded by people but yet isolated
I am tolerant but yet so angry
I am joyous but yet so sad
I am free but trapped within
I am successful but have failed
I am found but lost
I am here but nowhere to be seen
I am hopeful but in despair
I am a survivor but victimised
I am screaming my silent cries
I am weeping my dry tears
I am...
I know not who I am

A Mother's Lesson

She taught me how to love and be loved
She taught me that it is OK to cry
To show your emotions

She taught me that beauty comes from within
And is all around us
If we just open our eyes to it

She taught me that it is OK to fail
To make mistakes
To not always have to be right

She taught me that life is for the living
And death is not the end
But just a transitioning phase

She taught me that although I get older
I am still her son
Her child and baby from a foregone year

She taught me that respect is a two way street
She taught me that to hurt within is to feel alive
She taught me that grey skies are as beautiful as clear blue ones

But most of all she taught me that I am me
And to be proud of who I am
A mother's lesson that never ends

Mother

The touch of your smile is ever present whilst absent
Your perfume scent lingers in the midnight air
Our hearts parted but united in grief
Time never still but yet paused
Momentary lapses of the mind
As I reach out to call you
Empty arms outstretched
Caressing yesteryear's vapours
Nature's call to arms
The Mother who gives life
She claims you back to the soil
Where once you strolled
In your arms my life sprung forth
And in my arms your life ceased
You now live inside of me
As I once lived within you
Our hearts beat as one
Mother and child
Child and mother
Never parted
Life's continuum
Mother

The Garden Bench

In my garden there lies an empty bench
Where we would have sat and talked
You'd tell me how beautiful the garden is
How majestic the tree frames the skyline
Even in the depth of winter against the grey clouds,
You'd say there is beauty in everything
That darkness is only there to complement the light,
Sadness to elevate joy, tears to enhance laughter,
Your presence in this life is not measured by what you do
But rather the enormity of the void you leave behind,
Every day I miss you but some days more than others,
I grieve not your passing but the stillness of your voice,
My senses play tricks as I see you momentarily,
Hear you whisper to me or smell the sweet scent of your comfort,
But for now we will whisper quietly to one another,
I will still share my dreams and thoughts with you,
The winds will come and carry them to you,
And as the seasons change, the years go by,
The bench will still reside in my garden
Where we can talk momentarily with one another,
Missing you but thankful for the abundance of memories left behind,
Today was not a good day but rather a great one, thank you!

WAXING GIBBOUS

Life

When the noise stops
The silence intrudes
When the eyes steady
The lines are blurred
When the tears dry
The heart pines
When the hands steady
The legs implode
When the vision fades
The scent lingers
When you let go
The heart stops
When the sun sets
Life's shadow fades

Knock at the Door

He knocks at the door, you hide
Close your eyes, hold your breath, he will soon be gone
But patiently he waits, no hurry to move on
Why now, why must he call, I am not finished I am not complete

He arrived at birth and has bided his time
Debts to pay, ferrymen to transact with
I am not ready, you must come back

But still he stands there in the shadow of the street light outside your
door
His figure brumous in its stature
Your senses are aroused as you smell his ever presence
I am not ready you must come back

Eighty summers he has watched over you
Many times he knocked but you were not in
Tonight you are home the waiting is over for him

It's time to say your goodbyes, it's time to move on
No pain, no hurt, no sadness, just everlasting peace
Now it is my turn to hold and caress your hand
To still your fears, to reassure you all will be fine

27

I brush your hair, place my fingers gently across your emaciated cheek
I hold in my arms, your ever frail body no longer plump with life
You whisper "I love you son" and I respond as always, "I love you too"

The journey has ended, it's time to stop the fight
Sleep now, be not afraid, pain can no longer hurt you
Spread your wings and soar high, the door has now closed

Frozen Out

Arms outstretched
Emptiness embraced
Windows stained by hands
Seeking warmth of touch
Only shrill of coldness found
Eyes meet
Hearts ache
Journeyed faces look back
Chaperoned by loneliness
Self-isolation
Solitary confinement
Time crawls
Silence laboured
Eyes close
Freedom

The Emotionally Constipated Male

Firm of grip, virile and strong
Wisdom beyond their years or so they imply
The rock that brings the calm
Unstoppable in their pursuit of glory
The heartbeats within rarely skipping
The eyes stare vacantly into the abyss of constipated love
The chiselled look, the six pack
The way they stand and gaze into oblivion
Lips never quiver, eyes never water, voice never trembles
Emotions securely locked away
Laughter must be loud and hard
Where is the gentle touch?
The melting of the snowman
How to unlock the inner child
That disappeared so many moons ago
He is in there
He wails to be released
From this emancipation of love and tenderness
He too wants to giggle
Smile from within
Acknowledge his feelings openly
But the emotional constipated male wins out

The Lost Child

Time drags itself stumbling across the floor
Hours fumble as they dissipate into the dawn
Another late night or should that be early morn
My mind restless weighing heavy with fears
I drain the swamp of inevitability
But fears creep back into the very void I create
My eyes grow heavy as my heart is laden down
Consumed with the enormity of my thoughts
To my total enslavement of utter uselessness
I wriggle motionless in my bed
A prisoner of my own being
The epicentre of the self-indulgent child
She knows me no more, a stranger to her memories
Unrecognising the stranger as she looks in the mirror
Shedding tears for my father
As she strains to recognise his familiar face
Hurt, anger, frustration, anxiety, despair
These are the vocabulary of my thoughts
She soothed me through my childhood sleepless nights
As she cradled me in her arms
Now it is my turn to sooth away her bogeymen
I wrap my arms around her whilst rocking her to sleep
As I brush her hair, touch her face
Her eyes strain for recognition of this familiar face before her
A child lost in absent memories
A mother imprisoned within a lost world

31

No parole, no escape, simply existence
I plead for termination of sentence
My pleads are granted now I am the lost child

White Noise

The never ending white noise of this world
Fills the voids within the crevices of our being
That once resided for humanity
We have capitulated our social responsibility
In favour of the blue light of social media

Where 'Likes' are more important than empathy
Virtual friends are gathered like collectable cards
In favour of lasting friendships

Longevity is measured in terms of media traction
Rather than endurance throughout time
The world is closing in, becoming smaller
But yet we have never been so far apart

Communication is happening all around
But no one is talking, no one is listening
Nor present in the moment actively engaging
We are in danger of overcrowded isolation

Our thoughts are locked deep within
Never allowed to see the light of day
As to do so may impact on our Following
We'd rather only show our true selves
Through filters and touch-ups
But never bare naked our soul

The Dark Side Of Silence

The positivity bunny rabbits are bouncing all around
Quick to launch in with their never ending enthusiasm
Along with positive slogans without contemplating
Your needs, anxieties or suffering
Everything can be cured with a meme evangelistic quote

Weakness is not tolerated in this world
Of soft filters and touch-ups
Your suffering is their memento
As they collect the injured souls
Like reward stamps to promote their self-importance

Where to find solitude in this white noise of life
How to switch the noise off to find inner contentment
Without the need of notification alerts

To go back to basics, but what are basics
I need my soul to heal, I need my mind to be at peace
I need my eyes to close and lockout the white noise

Awkward Silence

Darkness descends as light dissipates till morning
Like fireflies, street lights flicker
The screeching sound of traffic is silenced
Footsteps upon pavements are no longer heard
A deafening silence has visited our surroundings

The sound of school children playing has been vanquished
Swings sway to the rhythm of the wind in abandoned playgrounds
No skipping, no chasing, no screeches of delight
The scratched knees have healed

Anxiety, apprehension, tearfulness approach
The isolation of our thoughts are overwhelming
We reacquaint with the image in the mirror
Their eyes somehow seem older now
As their brow droops
The joy of life has become a burden

Loved ones die in loneliness
No hand to hold, no farewell hug
No familiar voice to send them on their journey
A kiss on the cheek, a last good-bye
All stolen

We no longer count sheep rather the number of dead
Our lifetime has become redefined
Our impermanence revoked

The Dark Side Of Silence

Our strength is now our weakness
Our inner thoughts become our obsessions

We look out of our isolation cubicles, captives to nature
We are now the caged specimens as birds fly by our widows
Flowers shoot out of the ground mocking our state of confinement
Trees awaken from their slumber as buds unravel their splendour
Nature is at peace, it is at one with itself
It has become the constant in our lives

Time is our companion as it gnaws away
We are cocooned in an awkward silence
A silence of our inner selves where our fears lie
Strength lies within those fears through acceptance
As compassion shines through hope seeps in
Like the trees awakening from their slumber we will too
Our roots will be firmer and the turbulent winds of change
No longer will they uproot us but rather we shall sway
As our outstretched arms welcome our loved ones in

It will be a time of joy, a time of reconnection
Tears shall flow as heartbeats skip
The tactile feel of touching their hand
The awkward silence will be vanquished
The sound of children playing shall return
But till that day we will befriend that silence
As we await the reunion of humanity

The Fabric Of Life

I am not a simple man with simple thoughts
They are as disjointed and erratic as my reasoning
My complexities lie deep engrained within my fabric
My thread spun on the spinning wheel of life
Woven through the loom as the weft of my encounters are
intertwined
With the warp of my life
The shuttle moves through the fabric of my existence
Like an ancient Greek boustrophedon inscription chiselled into my
birthstone
I have nothing of worth to give the world
Except for my inner thoughts etched into my soul through my
encounters
Their eclectic reasoning's are as intricate as the cells that form my
outer carcass
Like a snake I shall shed that skin one day
To be reborn free from the scars I have endured in battle
I look for no sympathy or empathy from you
Nor do I seek retribution on those who cast the mould I have been
imprisoned in
The cast is now cracked, the inner sanctum exposed to the elements
As the light of hope seeps through
The cobbled road on which my bare feet thread has not yet ended
The end is never in sight
Rather it will appear out of the mist of uncertainty
As the heat from life's comforters expose it

37

One day raising that veil revealing the end
Then all shall be silent
All that will remain are those exposed thoughts of my life
Where the critics shall feverishly gorge themselves on their naivety
But my ears will be deafened to their denunciation
As my fabric becomes unravelled caught on the rusty nail of their
crucifix

Empty Chairs

Empty chairs at the breakfast table
Overcast shadows in family portraits
Your loss is the nation's grief
We knew not who they were but mourn their passing
The expediency of their exit from this world was too soon
Their laughter, their exuberance for life snuffed out
Their names rest on our lips
Our words of sympathy are inadequate
Where is Joyce, Yeats, Kavanagh or Heaney?
Our masters of literary genius to mould our suffering to verse
We are abandoned by all, we grope in the vacuum for succour
Mother Ireland weeps the loss of her young sons and daughters
Never to see the sun rise and glistened in their eyes
The sun has set, now darkness sets in as silence descends
It's time to bid our final farewell
Oíche Mhaith a chroí

This poem is dedicated to the memory of those young Irish students who died in the tragic Berkeley accident.

Misplaced Heart

I step into your world
The scent of the jacaranda hanging wistfully in the air
As I drive along with my car window down inhaling your presence
My eyes feasting upon the colour of your rainbow nation
The clicks of their tongue proclaiming my arrival
The sounds of nature's harmony emulate the orchestra of life
The birthplace of Madiba, Biko and Tambo
Their legacy outliving their ideology
Where to love is a rite of passage
The redness of your soil leaves a footprint
Embedded upon my misplaced heart
As I mourn my departure from your embrace
To return to my homeland I ache for
The warmth of your embrace
The love you bestowed upon me
South Africa the cradle of humankind

FULL MOON

Mother Nature Has Taken My Mother

Mother Earth gave me a mother
And time is stealing her memories from her
Now I have her memories within me
But time is stealing my mother from me
Life goes on as time reaps the fruits of her labour
I selfishly pray for time to hasten
To release my father from his prison duties
But death has no parole board
Or acquittal for compassionate leave
You have stolen her from us
Yet she is here but not all at the same time
Oh how cruel you are Mother Nature
You call yourself our nurturer
I curse and damn you but I love you too
Now her sentence is served
She is released from her solitary confinement
My heart is heavy with the guilt
I sought no extension of time
Rather I celebrated her release
Mother Nature has taken my mother

Snowflakes

I may never smell your scent
Nor feel your caress
The warmth of your embrace shall escape me
The sound of your voice I'll never hear

But don't think of me as lost
I am still your child
Your breath carried in a different dimension
I am here, I am with you

Reach out your arms
As the breeze envelops you it is my embrace
As the rain runs down your face they are my tears
As the snowflakes melt on your lips it is my kiss

Your skipped heartbeats are stolen by me
Caught breaths are captured by me
Carry my name with you as I carry yours
I am still your child…

This poem is dedicated to the memory of Asha Reilly, born sleeping on 08-MAR-2008 who was too fragile for this world.

Rose Petal

A rose petal falls
Silently descending
Resting upon the soil
From where it's life sprung forth
As it does so
Performing Ravel's Bolero
No trace of impact apparent
But rather it's lingering scent
Encapsulating our senses
It's perfume pure and sweet
Velvet like skin to the touch
Staining our souls with its beauty
Its life blossomed too early
Exposed to the morning frost
Now it lies listless upon the hardened soil
Awaiting the thaw
From the glistening sun
It's beauty captured in time
Never to grow old
Our eternal rose petal

This poem is dedicated to the memory of Asha's younger sister Amber Reilly, born 09–FEB–2010 and joined her older sister on 15–FEB–2010, sisters forever, their beauty and innocence frozen in time.

Rebirth

When the silence descends upon the grave of memories
As the pining of the heart stretches beyond the perimeter of tolerance
Whilst the reverberation of anxiety overpowers intellectual rational

When eyes swollen with enormity of grief are buried deep within
The heaviness of movement weighed down by the inertia of lost love
The ever deafening sound of silence consumes you from within

Darkness cannot come swiftly enough
All seems lost within the quagmire of unobtainable happiness
Life is lost in the wilderness of empathy never to be found in apathy

The bleakness of the futility of love scattered across the wastelands of
hope
In the distance comes the murmuring cries of rebirth
Entering our world of darkness shinning the light of hope

Their innocence pure, their love infectious
The touch of their skin, the scent of their being
Life's continuum never ending

For in momentary death there is rebirth
Through our pain we discover healing
And through healing we find ourselves

Stillness

Your smile
Your touch
Smoothness of your skin
Your lingering scent
The beauty you behold
Breaths you steal
Emotions you evoke
The stirring of life within
Unconditional love
Light arms
Heavy hearts
Skipped heartbeats
Untold stories
Never ending sunsets
Unseen dawns
Stillness

Unconditional Love

Your scent, your convulsions of laughter,
Your exuberance for life glistening in your eyes
The gentleness of your touch, the freshness of your skin
Your quivering lip, the purity of your tears
The innocence of your being, the magnitude of your presence
The unconditional love, the enormity of your trust

Happiness is the epicentre of your presence
Life is within your grasp, goals have no boundaries
Nothing is impossible and everything is possible
No boundaries, no opinions, no falsehoods
Your thoughts are pure, your intentions innocent
Your life is our reward, our gift, our pleasure

You place your hand in mine and look deep into my soul
You puncture my thoughts of darkness with the brightness of your light
You cast no shadow as you step inside of mine
That laughter, those flinching eye lids, the fullness of your cheeks
You are the irrefutable evidence of my existence
You are life, life is you, and we are the same but not

Your journey is beginning mine is waning
You fear nothing, despise no one, and are tolerant of all
You are my future, I am your past
Our lives interwoven through love,
Parted through grief
Heartbeats still but never stopped

Call My Name

The innocence in your smile
The joy of life in your eyes
The scent of your soul
The infectiousness of your life

Your hand rests in mine
Your skin so soft
Nestled in the arch of my arm
Our lives are joined

Your first steps and words
Engraved in my thoughts
Just to be present in your presence
To feel that exuberance for life

We share moments
They are my gift to you
For times that lie ahead
When my absence will be felt

But never grieve
We had each other
I am never far
Simply call my name

Mind Games

Another year has passed, another candle absent on the cake
You are not here to blow them out, your absence ever present
The sound of your laughter, your crooked smile
Snuffed out like the candles on the cake

No one to guide me, no one to chastise me
Momentarily I hear you call my name
I see you in the crowds, I sense your presence
Only to lose you once again to mind games

How I long for that momentary lapse
To be still, present and last forever
The hunger of the loss, the despair of my aching heart
The selfishness of the mourning son

I am a grown man, a husband, a father, a Pappy
But my identity is moulded in being your son
Now it is lost and shattered
I am at sea with my emotions
As the evening swell overpowers me

I visit your resting place, touch your picture
My fingers travel within the chiselled inscription
I long to hold you in my arms, to feel the warmth of your caress
The security of your embrace

49

The woe of your absence will never pass
But neither will the memories
You have given more than I could ask
I love you now as much in death as I did in life
You are my blood, my breath, my being

WANING GIBBOUS

Lost Souls

Lost souls surfing the waves
Balance delicately controlled
Outstretched arms
Legs anchored
Feet poised
Navigating the sea of life
Beacons of hope in distance
Life crashing on the rocks
The swell engulfs their hopes
But they ride the crest
Calmer water lies on the horizon
Balance to be restored

Collateral Damage

The sound of children's laughter
Drowned out by falling stars
Heartbeats race as fear sets in
Tear tracks form upon my cheeks
The weight of revenge pushing down
My chest crushing under the strain
Frantically I reach out to find you
In the darkness of lost humanity
My fingers intertwine into yours
Your skin is cold to the touch
Gasping for air I cry out your name
But my lungs are bereft of oxygen
Closing my eyes I see you knelt before me
Arms outstretched welcoming me home
I run into your arms for sanctuary
You stand and we walk hand in hand
I momentarily pause to look back
Only to see my outer body
Strewn motionless upon the rubble of hatred
As it's pulled from the debris
Wrapped in a blanket of lost hope
Gently they lower my limp body
Resting me delicately upon the ground
The soil of my birth place, my homecoming
I seem so small but for four I was tall
Cries can be heard as people gather

Another casualty of conflict
Collateral damage is my epitaph
A victim of failed diplomacy
A statistic of an unjust war
One less person to displace
The justifiable price of protectionism
As the persecuted turn persecutors
We are a people displaced in this time
Prayers will be said, candles lit
Voices will rise up to say my name
I am Collateral Damage

Young Poet

Stoic he stands before us
Poised to take flight
The words flow effortlessly
His eyes fixated on our soul
Exposing our hidden wounds
As he eloquently recites
His young years defy his ability
The dawn of hope rises
As he takes us by the hand
To the land of poets
Casey, Heaney, Kavanagh are his peers
Their words lying dormant on the page
Awaiting the breath of life
Through his spoken words
He carries them across the ocean of life
Resting delicately upon our souls
As they touch our lives
Through gentle murmuring in our ears
Ink stained pages become life's charter
As words collide, reverberating through our body
The poets lay peacefully
Smiling down upon their future son

This poem is dedicated to Alex Molloy, an upcoming Irish poet who has already won awards at the young age of twelve.

Intrepid Explorers

Mum how many more days
Mum when will they be here?
Mum where will they sleep?

The noise of excitement
The anticipation of the cousins' arrival
How can I sleep, where will we sleep?
Will we sleep, do we need to sleep?

Oh mum are you sure they are coming?
I cannot see their car
Mum hurry up where are they?
Mum, they're here!

Greeted with an exuberance of disbelief
"Wait till you see what I got"
A tsunami of pent up excitement
Unleashed like a whirlwind of hysteria

The ever presence of a single little person's voice
Culminated into an orchestra of feverish enthusiasm
They have become the three amigos
Never to be parted from one another's side

Raymond Poole

The house is filled with an energy
It transcends any Wembley final
The title championship cup to be played tonight
Is that of everlasting friendship

They move like a herd of wildebeest
Across the African plains
As they go to infinity and beyond

Their time travel machine brings them to places
Where no human inhabitants have visited before
Discovering new planets in the galaxy of forget-me-nots
Exploring the depths of the ocean floor

But now silence descends upon these intrepid explorers
Side by side, top to tail like sardines
Snuggly nestled in their cocoon of fantasy land
They sleep dreaming of times gone by, adventures yet to come

For tomorrow they venture back in time to a prehistoric World
After all becoming five is indeed a milestone of magnitude
proportion

This poem was dedicated to Mathew Molloy on his fifth birthday.

A Dyslexic's Poem

I now every know and then I get my know's mixed up
I see the ways of my errors in mirrors
Then dares the horse thrown over the fence for food
As along comes Missus does be and her do be chiselers
It's being awhile before I've been sane
But the curse of the silent letter
Along width the infringement of tenses
Mascaraed eye's before e except after sea
Sow many complications in my dyslexic head
As the tree threes sway in unison
The breath of the task is not lost
However I now as time passes
For yesterday's tomorrow is know
I will simply smile and say I now

THIRD QUARTER

My Land

The Atlantic turbulent skyline
Frames the rustic night setting
As the tree's outstretched branches
Awaken from its hibernation
A blanket of silence wraps mystically
Across the slumbering land
My feet anchored in the soil of
Cú Chulainn, Grainne and the children of Lir
From which I was born
And where I shall return one day
Rory's screeching guitar
Reverberating across the kingdom
While Phillo's seductive smile
Draws us in to his town
Damo tells tales of the Choctaw Nation
As Glen and the boys Revelate
The sound beats of my childhood reverberate
As I drag a stick along the railings
To the beat of Bloody Sunday
With the sun on my back
Chewing upon the long stem grass
No cares, no worries just adolescence contemplation
The heart skips a beat as she looks back
Shadows from the cathedral of life
Attempt to darken the spirit of freedom
But the sun wins out as pillars Collapse and Governments implode

Raymond Poole

The people's voice rises up
The cries of suffering and lost hopes
Are carried upon the lips of empathy
Women emerge from the shadows
No longer shackled to the hypocrisy
Of a male dominated constitution
Claiming their right to sovereignty
Of their bodies and to the right of equality
Mistakes are forgiven but neglect never
Too many suffered at the hand of authority
The wind of change flows throughout the land
Ideologies exposed as the band aid is ripped
From the festering skin of apathy
Rainbows no longer vaporise
As their flags flurry in the skyline
Once shamed and pilloried for their beliefs
They now stand tall in the presence of the new dawn
Where the snowflakes showed their strength
This is my land

Warrior Woman

She's gentle, thoughtful & elegant
A daughter, mother, sister and aunt
From the caverns within her soul emits calm
Her story too familiar
Her wounds masked by her beauty
She seeks no favour
Never in flight, always standing her ground
Anchored to the soil
Lips pierced from thorns bitten
She is a combatant mother
She is a Warrior Woman

The Hummingbird

She is perched upon the branch of self-loathing
Inside the cage of on demand performance
Her gatekeeper never rewarding upon song
Never satisfied with her performance
His firm grip breaking her delicate wings

She sat in isolation from tenderness, love and praise
Staring out from behind her prison bars over the horizon
Thoughts of freedom accompanied by self-belief seeping through
As self-expressionism nestled within her mind
Seasons only marked by the return of the Canadian geese
As they flew by the closed window of neglect
Time never standing still rather silently shuffling

He was the overseer of her neglectful existence
Taking pride in leaving the cage ajar
Never fearing her flight as he crushed her spirit
Knowing a mother would never abandon her chicks
She sang every day for his pleasure but never hers

Freedom came at a heavy price
The morning song abandoned her
Replaced by the cries of single parenthood
Her nest now made from broken promises
Intertwined with heartache but lined with hope
And soon her chicks would learn to fly

The Dark Side Of Silence

She now sits on a branch by the shoreline
Gazing out on the sea of life
Contemplating her journey and times gone by
Her voice has returned echoing sounds of joy
Her feathers plumb ready for flight
Soaring above she sets her own calendar
The Canadian geese still visit but their beauty now admired

The hummingbird now sings about life
As her songs fill the air with hope
Providing solace to those held captive in cages
This bird has flown the cage of her captivity
A rebirth is imminent as the dawn chorus awaits patiently her arrival

This poem is dedicated to Luna

Oh Catholic Ireland

Oh Catholic Ireland how you've fallen from grace
Overseeing the crucifixion of your daughters you hid away
Now a light shines brightly upon the septic flaws of your elders
The darkness of your soul reflected in your robes
As their bare hands scrubbed your sins away
Innocence robbed as society averted their gaze
Cries muffled by the sound of the rosary
Children discarded as the doors to Limbo remained ajar
Whispers on the streets
Judgements cast upon our daughters
As the perpetrators knelt and kissed the ring for a blessing
The umbilical cords were cut to deafening silence
Shame bestowed upon the innocent
Lifeless limbs discarded in a cesspit of guilt hidden from compassion
The hunters now become the hunted
Nowhere to hide in their conclave of virtue
Mother Ireland with outstretched arms cradles her stolen children
As society catches glimpses of those complicit in the mirror
Silence and averted glances no longer justifiable excuses
Our blood stained hands washed in the holy water of complicity
The children's voices have been heard
Their names carried upon our lips
Never to be forgotten they were born of this land
Our children need to sleep peacefully wrapped in dignity
As the empty arms of their mother's weigh heavy
Ireland once again lowers its head in shame
Oh Catholic Ireland where was your compassion

Ireland's Daughters

Her smiling eyes pierce your soul
Seeing your pain she reaches out
Her hand rests upon yours
Quietly spoken, her words soothe
Her presence ever comforting
Her touch reassuring
Her embrace caring
She is our Jeanne d'Arc
A warrior like no other
A champion of the people
Her battle scars lie deep
Her time is limited
It pauses momentarily
Whilst in her presence
As no clock is ticking
A woman born of this island
Rooted in its heritage
Rising up for those suffering
Navigating the political quagmire
Fending off the arrows of insult
Shielding the vulnerable
The people's daughter
We're indebted to her sacrifice
Her crucifixion publicly displayed
Alongside two hundred and twenty one crosses
Erected upon the hill of oversight

Raymond Poole

One by one
The sun sets slowly on them
As their shadows fade into the darkness
Only to be reborn under the moon lit sky
Resting their heads upon the soil
Their names etched in headstones
Their loss carved in the hearts of their loved ones
Their pain silenced
Their voices never
We shall whisper their names
As the wind of change carries them forward
Our eyes will meet once more
As they walk through our dreams
One last embrace
One final farewell
Our lives eternally interlaced
They are the dewy droplets
Captured by the morning sun
Creating the rainbows of hope
Ireland's daughters
Lost to political ineptness
Apologies too late
Our daughters, sisters, mothers and grandmothers
Codladh sámh!

*This poem is dedicated to Vicky Phelan and all those women caught up in
the cervical smear debacle.*

WANING CRESCENT

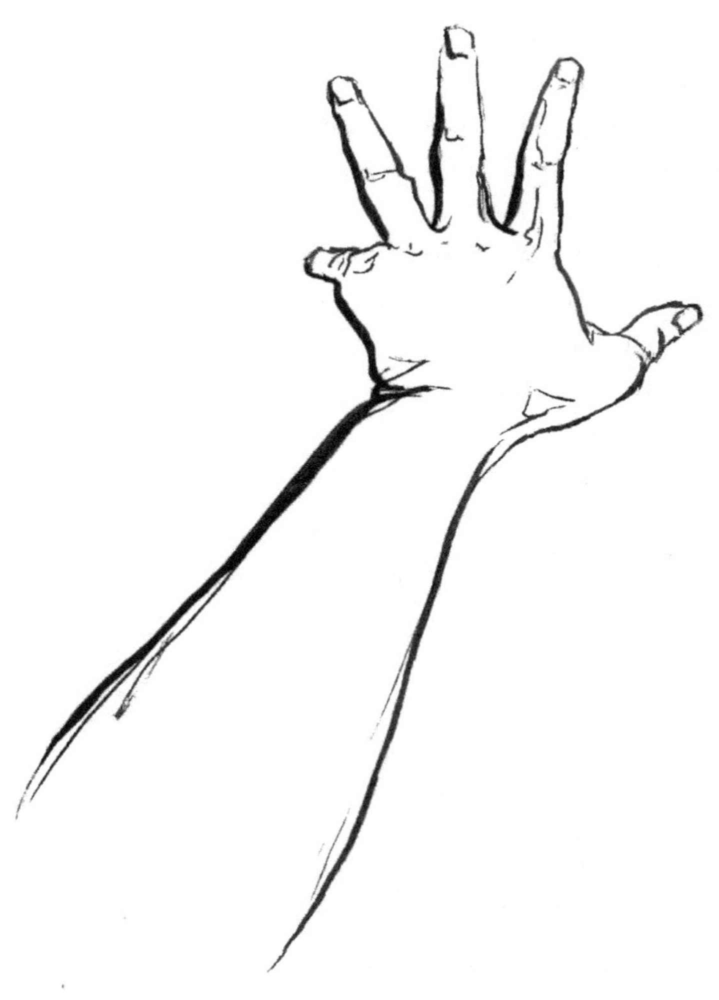

The Poet

Silently he fixates his stare
Gazing aimlessly out the window
Seeking inspiration of thought
At moments paused that may linger
Hanging from the silken thread of life
Weaving a web of miscomprehension
Only to perplex the critics
As they gorge on the inadvertent structure
Rhythm abandoned with collapsing form
Truth no longer camouflaged
Rather laid bare as in birth
Umbilical cord cut
As screeches of life reverberate
Upon the new dawn of forced reality
The echo chambers in the christening hall
Fall hollow in the famine of culpability
Pillars of faith implode
As atonement is foregone
While the sacrificial lamb
Lies motionless upon the alter
Blood red robes genuflect
Closing rank to blind the passing eye
The poet stains the blank page
With the black ink of life's journey
Stripping naked the starkness of lost souls
Poetry becomes the poet
As the shutters open on life's window

Where Is The Darkness?

Vice tightens as cranium contorts and twists
Vision distorted with images of bleeding flesh
Light descends with fierceness of a knight slaying his victim
Where is the sanctuary of darkness?
Sounds amplify to deafening decibels
Where is the tranquillity of darkness?
Body retracts to foetus position in search of refuge
Inner peace is dispersed amongst the embers of pain
Where is the solitude of darkness?
Tears flow from eyes in spasm in reflex to the gritting of the eye lids
The rustic jagged blades are scratched across the surface of the eyes
As the skull is penetrated from the rear with the piercing of a spear
Momentarily life is abandoned as pain prepares for its coup de foudre
Where is the darkness of my embryotic state?

Falling

As sound of silence deafens
Every breath is amplified
Crowded spaces appear in empty rooms
Strangers' reflections look out from mirrors
Inner thoughts explode
Imploding anxiety
Enormity of insignificance realised
Spiralling into the abyss
Laden down with weight of guilt
Outstretched hands
Hollow grasp
Falling

Eyes Closed

I'm tired looking you down
Your persistence is exhausting
Your presence unwanted
I walk the fine line
Stripped of my worth
My breath labours at your name
My, no our lives matter
Darkness is beckoning
Solitude at last
The insignificance of our lives restored
Eyes closed

Twits

A circle of friendship of unlikely occurrence
Their meeting accidental
No stars aligned, rather collided
Out of that debris of destruction
Emerged a friendship of hope
No Famous Five here, rather six orphans
Each walking along life's railway track
In parallel with no point of intersection
They had differing destinations
But unbeknownst to them a crossing lay ahead
Their tales are similar but different
Heartaches, illness and abuse
This is after all an Irish tale
But in this circle there is comfort
Calmness and strength
Their hearts now weigh less
From the weight of trauma
As each elevates the other
Under the darkness of the night sky
They light up one another's pathway
Their burdens no longer carried alone
Hurt and tragedy hasn't stopped calling
But rather when it knocks at their door
Six defiant faces now stare back
Only to be interrupted by skitting
Their destinations no longer important

Rather the journey is their focus
Time taken to pause and laugh loudly
They are the Twits

Shadow Dancing

Standing in the shadows
Hiding from my vulnerability
Fearful of the spotlight
Your songs came calling
As I shadow danced to their mysticism

A serendipitous meeting of lost souls
Your voice came across the airwaves
The hook within the tune was set
Your melancholic tone reeled me in
Suddenly my life was being unveiled

Out of that calm came a storm
A swell blinded by the horizon
Turbulent waters lay ahead
A safe harbour was sought
Your friendship guiding me in

Those dark lonely nights
Became a sanctuary to dark thoughts
As your music raised me up
Floating above the crowd
Waves of hope now washed over me
My aching body healed by the notes

Creativity grew out of despair
Self-doubt yielded to encouragement
The written words collided
As lost voices emerged
Through your constant presence of support

Now within those shadows
The orchestra tunes to my life's symphony
Hope takes despair by the hand
As they dance to their own tune
Entwined within the vines of life

Heartbeats skip as breaths pause
Unveiling the lost children
Hidden no more in the shadows
As the sun raises their heads
How much more you going to make of me

Amuse-Bouche

Grief

I awaken to the dawn of my emotions
Reaching out to touch you
You fade into the chasm of my grief
Never to be present
Till I too fade

Promise

When all is done
I shall be silent
My voice will fade into the wind
My image will become a blur
But my promise will remain

My Soul

As the shadow casts upon my soul
Whilst my breath is carried upon the wind
My memories are drowned amongst the rising tide

NEW MOON

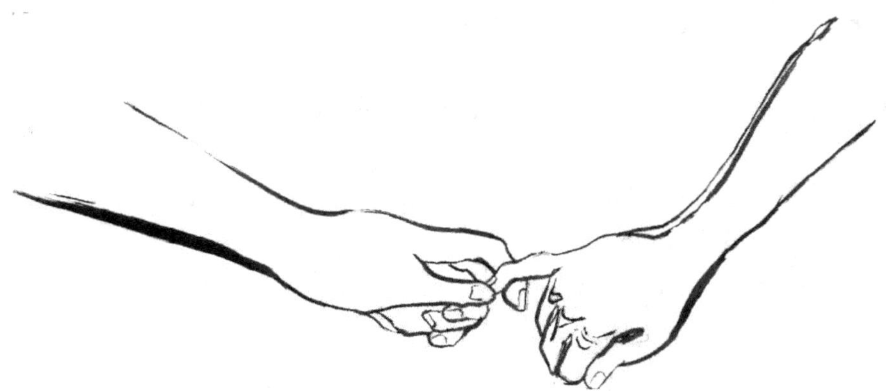

The Absent Lover

I am present but yet I am absent
My physical being lies here
But my inner soul has vacated
This emotionally constipated vessel

I long to hold you close
But now find I have built an invisible barrier
The barbed wire of my own deprived emotions
Is preventing the tender touch, the closeness
The emotional warmness and tenderness of your caress

I crawl into bed at night contemplating my existence, my journey
And feel void of all emotion
Overwhelmed by the never ending noise within
The voices, the images, the silent screams

What lies ahead for us, where do we go now?
How do we reignite that special love we have for each other
When will this all end, how can we survive this intrusion
This mistress that has entered our relationship
The unwanted third party

I am coping but yet I am not
I've neglected you for the sake
Of gathering my own sanity but to what price
We speak, you listen, and comfort me

The Dark Side Of Silence

But I am on the outside observing
When will I be present again?

So many questions, so few answers
Kind words, glances, nods of acknowledgement
They don't replace the emptiness I feel
The abandonment of my life, the war raging inside
The battles are easily won but the war is harder to overcome

Writing is the easiest bit, the words flow
The letters dance amongst the sheets
Colliding into a meaningful sentence
But they are oh so hard to say aloud
To admit to oneself how you truly feel
To hear those words aloud
That's the torture deep down within

How dare the world continue
Does it not realise the suffering contained within
Does it not hear the silent deep throated squeals for help?
The utter deprivation of humanity as we suffer
With dry tears streaming down our faces
So many suffering, too few listening

To listen, that is the thing, the art,
To keeps one's mouth shut and stay within the moment
But it's so hard to listen, so much easier to speak
To fill the silent void with incompatible sympathetic nonsense

Raymond Poole

This life, this debt we must pay to the paymaster
For something we never sought
Who are they to say who should suffer?
The so called all caring loving vapours of influential tormenters
Who gave them the right to righteousness?
Who are they to say what sin is and when life should end?

Close the door, leave the noise outside
Breathe slowly and release the angst of the inner turmoil
I shall return one day, be present once more in your life
Be present once more in your bed
Be the person you fell in love with
Be the partner you deserve
But for now I am the absent lover.

No Words

Your fingers weave through mine
No words are spoken, none needed
Acknowledgement of our love lies within our eyes
Thoughts of the abandonment of my presence intrude
As the nakedness of our love
Lies bare to the storm of my emotions
The hunger is real in this famine
The neglect of my advances
Strewn across the shattered glass
Where the silken thread of love frays
And snags on crushed hopes
Unravelling the fabric of our bond
Lust lies listless upon the bonnet
Of our car crash of emotions
No words just silent tears
As we mourn the death of intimacy
The bruises lie buried deep within
Invisible to the passing eye
Our smiles camouflage the loneliness
Emotions overcrowded by emptiness
Our love is as real as is the pain
No words...

Night Shadows

Under cover of darkness
My mind seeks sanctuary
Lying amongst the crevices of self-doubt
As the stained shadows seep through
Regurgitating the abscess of my past
Suppressing my liberation

The light that once shone
Creating the shadow of my life
No longer glows
Rather it flickers
Till eventually it's snuffed out

I silently lay down beside you
Here we lie as one
Only complete when together
I cup your hand in mine
United, entwined and solidified

No words are ever said
None are ever needed
Our breathing becomes one
Our lives inextricably joined
Morning will come, darkness disintegrates
The night shadows will vaporise

Acknowledgements

Once again I want to say a huge thanks of gratitude to Karl Smyth, for the book cover design. This is the third book cover that Karl has designed for me and I am deeply appreciative of his support.

A word of thanks to my publisher, Orla O'Kelly, who once again has done an amazing job.

To Philip Nolan for capturing those misspellings, punctuation etc. You are a very kind and generous person, thank you!

To Gareth O'Callaghan, not just for the Foreword but the friendship Paula and you have extended to Selena and I. It is deeply appreciated.

The sequence in which the poems appear in the book were done under the skilful and talented eye of Carolin. Without her this would simply have been a mess, thank you my friend.

To my primary school teacher, Patrick Kavanagh of St Damien's Primary School, Greenhills. At a time when I needed comfort, safe hands and sanctuary, you gave it to me.

To Peter McVeigh, who not only continues to lift me up when I am down, but allows me to use him as a conduit for my creativity.

To Zoe Maher, my amazing niece who put images to my words. You are an incredibly gifted individual and I am privileged to have your artwork accompany my poems. Thank you so much, xx.

Finally, I cannot close off this section without acknowledging the unwavering support of my wife, Selena, who finds herself a widow to my writings. She allows me the space to stain the pages, the encouragement to continue when I stall, and provides me with a belief that I can do this when I doubt I have the ability. I love you xx

To all those who have recorded videos reading my poems, I truly thank you for breathing life into my dormant words. Poetry only comes to life when the words are spoken aloud. To see and listen to these recording simply visit my website at www.raymondpoole.com.

If you wish to follow Raymond on social media, you may do so on Twitter at @Aladinsane40 or on Instagram at poole_raymond.

Raymond is always interested in feedback so please reach out to him and let him know what you thought of his poetry.

www.ingramcontent.com/pod-product-compliance
Lightning Source LLC
Chambersburg PA
CBHW070507170726
48291CB00008B/2691